Cecilia McDowall

A SONG FOR ST CECILIA

vocal score

OXFORD
UNIVERSITY PRESS

OXFORD
UNIVERSITY PRESS

Great Clarendon Street, Oxford OX2 6DP,
United Kingdom

Oxford University Press is a department of the University of Oxford.
It furthers the University's objective of excellence in research, scholarship,
and education by publishing worldwide. Oxford is a registered trade mark of
Oxford University Press in the UK and in certain other countries

First published 2025

Impression: 1

ISBN 978–0–19–358026–8

Music origination by Ralph Woodward

Printed in Great Britain on acid-free paper by
Caligraving Limited

Commissioned by The Bar Choral Society, Greg Morris, Music Director

A Song for St Cecilia

Kate Wakeling

CECILIA McDOWALL

Duration: 10.5 mins

Printed in Great Britain

* pronounced Cec*ee*lia

Let_ the word_ be writ-ten in let-ters of

Let_ the word_ be writ-ten in let-ters of

Let_ the word_ be writ-ten in let-ters of

Let_ the word_ be writ-ten in let-ters of

Ped.

gold._____ She is Ce-ci - li - a, Ce-ci - li - a, she

gold._____ She is Ce-ci - li - a, Ce-ci - li - a, she

gold._____ She is Ce-ci - li - a, Ce-ci - li - a, she

gold._____ She is Ce-ci - li - a, Ce-ci - li - a, she

Man.

is Ce-ci-li - a,___ Ce - ci - li - a,___ she is Ce-ci - - - li-

Ped.

Man.

and her heart_____ was clean as___ the

and her heart_____ was clean as___ the

li - ly, and her *cre - - aunce sweet and clear_____ as__ the morn - ing.

li - ly, and her *cre - - aunce sweet and clear_____ as__ the morn - ing.

as the li - ly,

as the li - ly,

* creaunce = belief

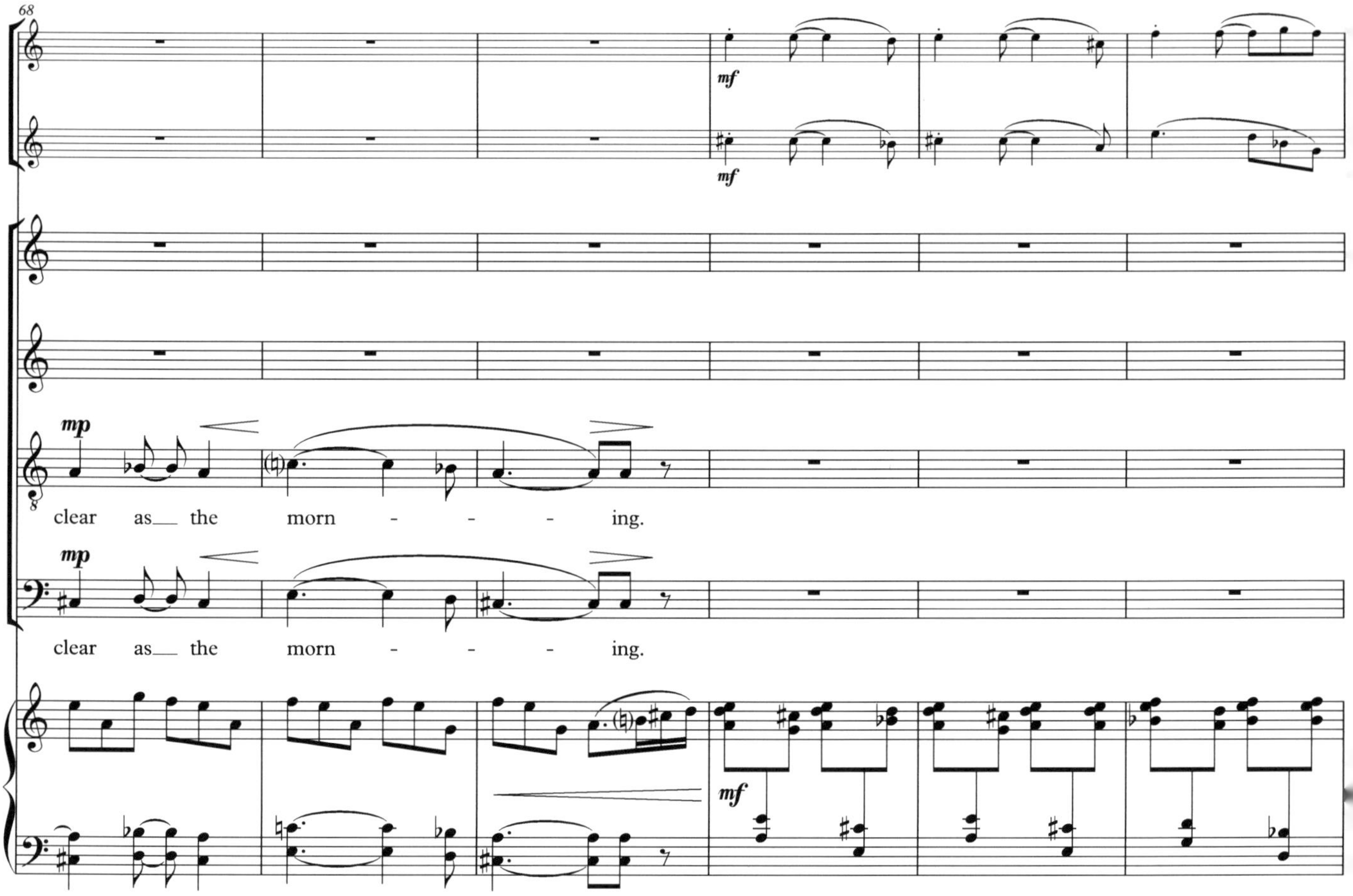
68
mp
clear as the morn - - - ing.
mp
clear as the morn - - - ing.
mf
mf
mf

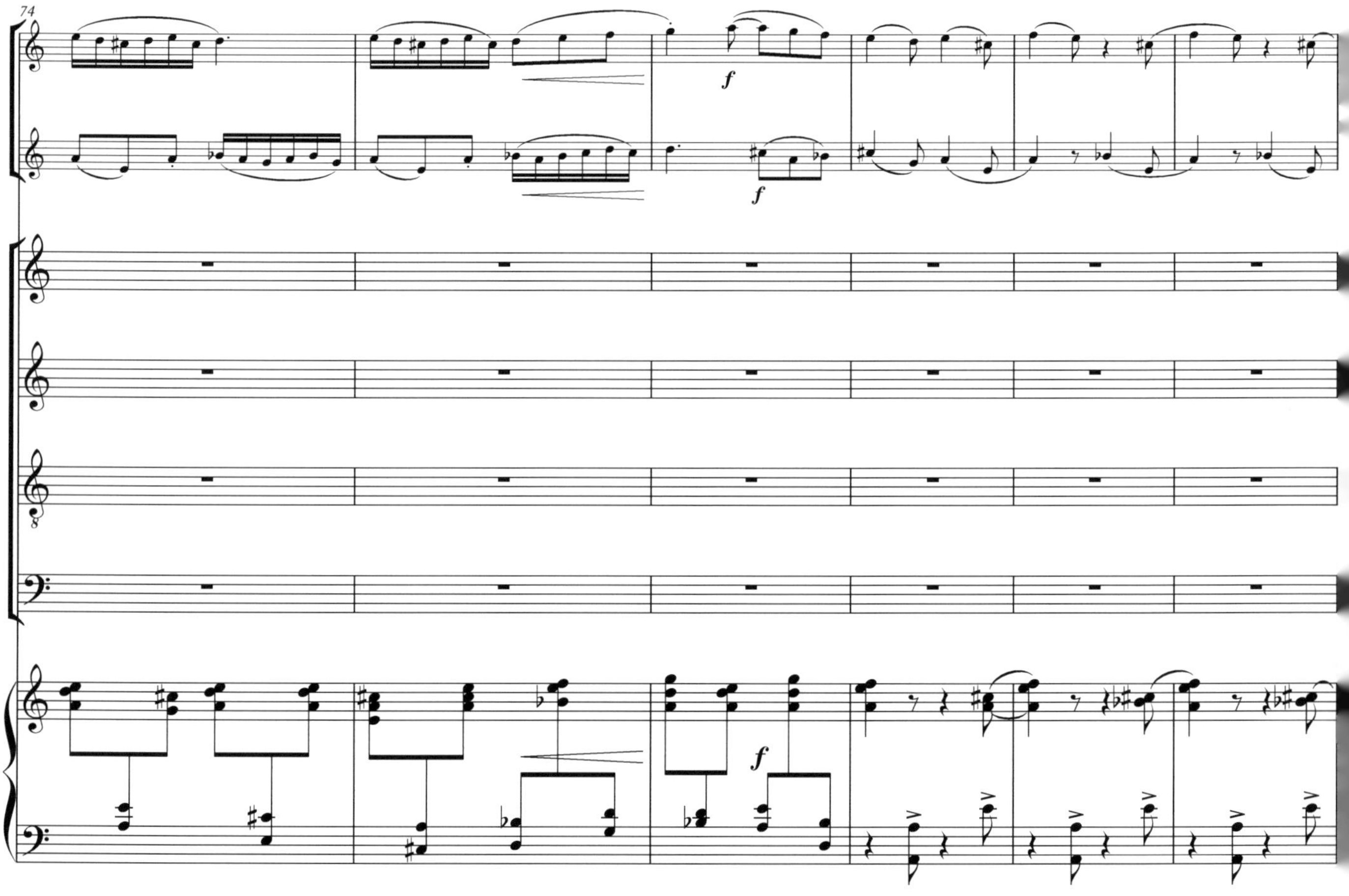
74
f
f
f

It is from Ce-ci-li-a we learn the great pe-ti-tion,

It is from Ce-ci-li-a we learn the great pe-ti-tion,

It is from Ce-ci-li-a we learn

It is from Ce-ci-li-a we learn

the great pe-ti-tion of me - lo - dy,____ of me-lo-dy;____

the great pe-ti-tion of me - lo - dy,____ of me-lo-dy;____

great pe-ti-tion, the great pe-ti-tion of me - lo - dy,____ of me-lo-dy;____

great pe-ti-tion, the great pe-ti-tion of me - lo - dy,____ of me-lo-dy;____

Ped.

Man.

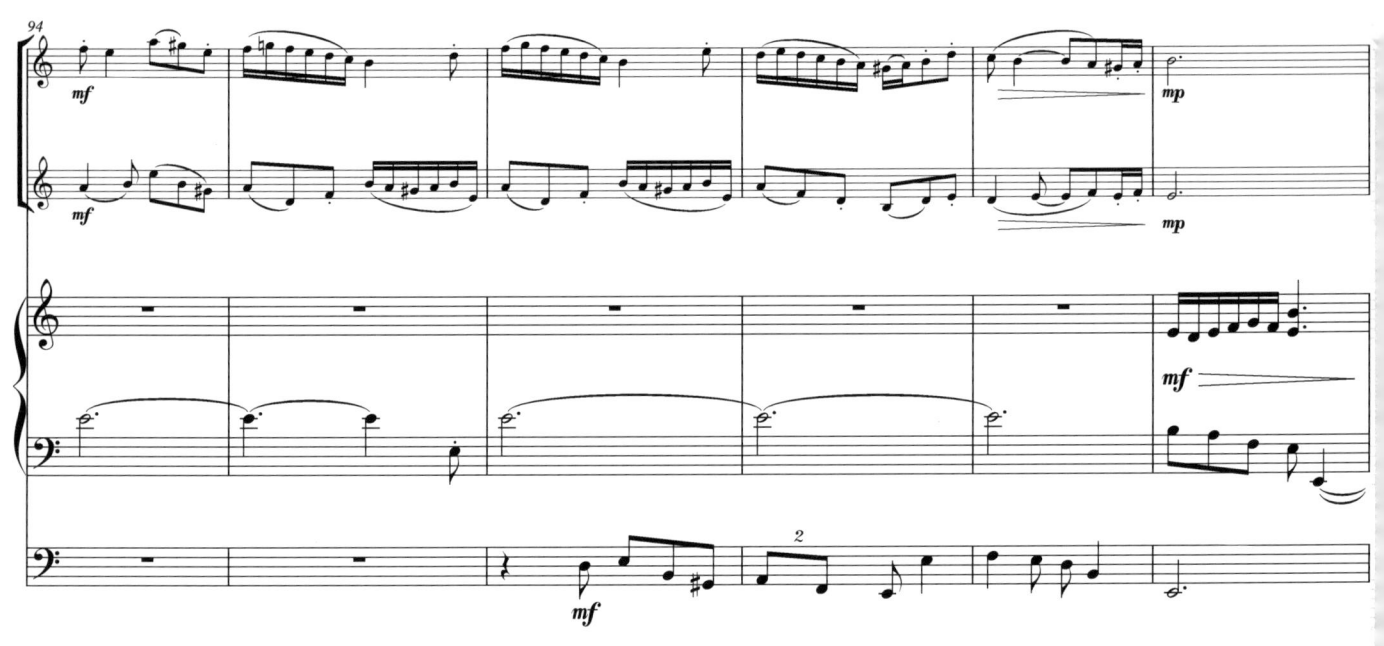

94
mf
mf
mf
mp
mp
mf
2

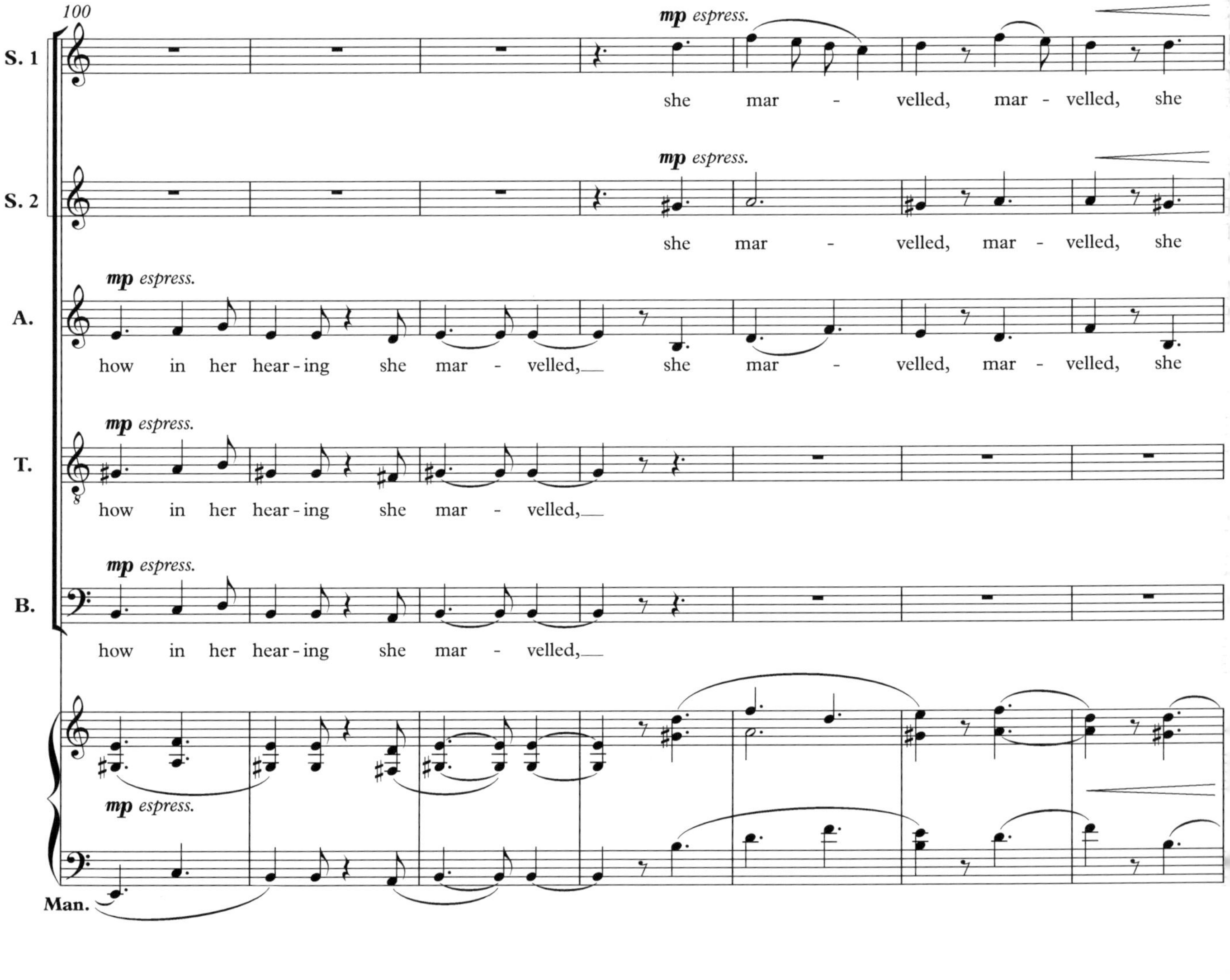
100
S. 1
mp espress.
she mar - velled, mar - velled, she
S. 2
mp espress.
she mar - velled, mar - velled, she
A.
mp espress.
how in her hear-ing she mar - velled, she mar - velled, mar - velled, she
T.
mp espress.
how in her hear-ing she mar - velled,
B.
mp espress.
how in her hear-ing she mar - velled,
mp espress.
Man.

will, in her will.

will, in her will.

will, in her will.

will, in her will.

will, in her will.

Man.

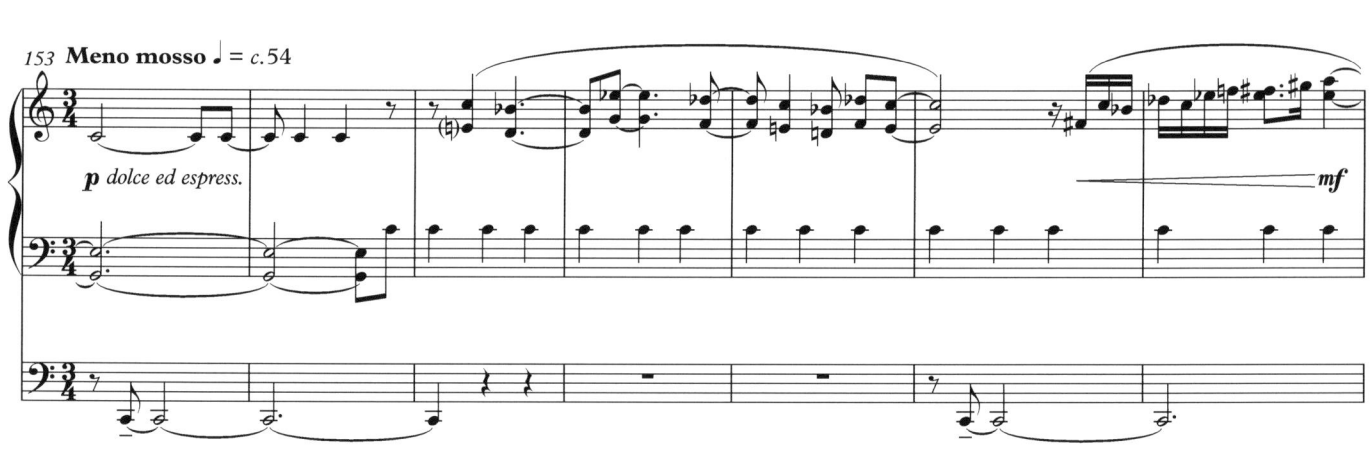

For the hear-ing of the

Man.

And in that burn - ing cor - ner of

And in that burn - ing cor - ner of

mp dolce

me-lo-dy, she found grace___ and bliss___ and life and death,___ life_ and death.

me-lo-dy, she found grace___ and bliss___ and life and death,___ life_ and death.

of me-lo-dy,

of me-lo-dy,

life___ and death.___

life___ and death.___

She suf - fered but her ve - ry truth was joy ... for she

She suf - fered but her ve - ry truth was joy ... for she

She suf - fered but her ve - ry truth was joy

She suf - fered but her ve - ry truth was joy

of light, in arms of light, of light.

of light, arms of light, of light.

of light, arms of light, of light.

of light, arms of light, of light.

of light, arms of light, of light.